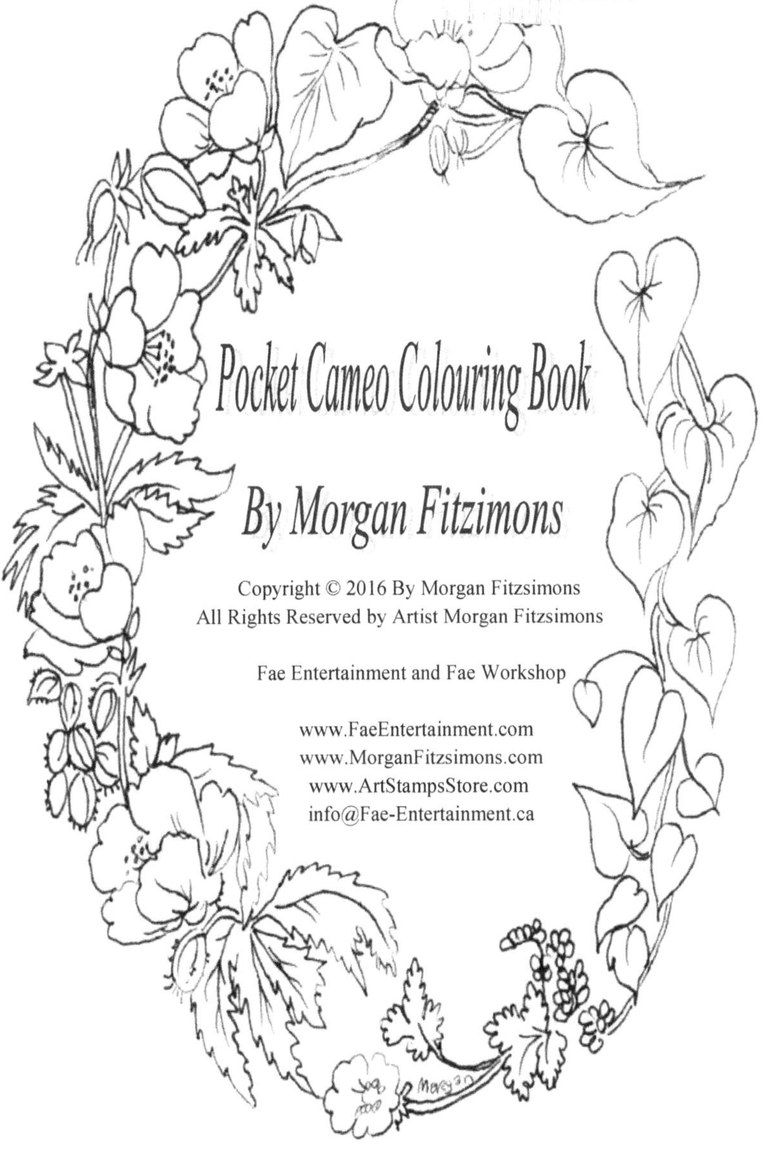

Pocket Cameo Colouring Book

By Morgan Fitzimons

Copyright © 2016 By Morgan Fitzsimons
All Rights Reserved by Artist Morgan Fitzsimons

Fae Entertainment and Fae Workshop

www.FaeEntertainment.com
www.MorganFitzsimons.com
www.ArtStampsStore.com
info@Fae-Entertainment.ca

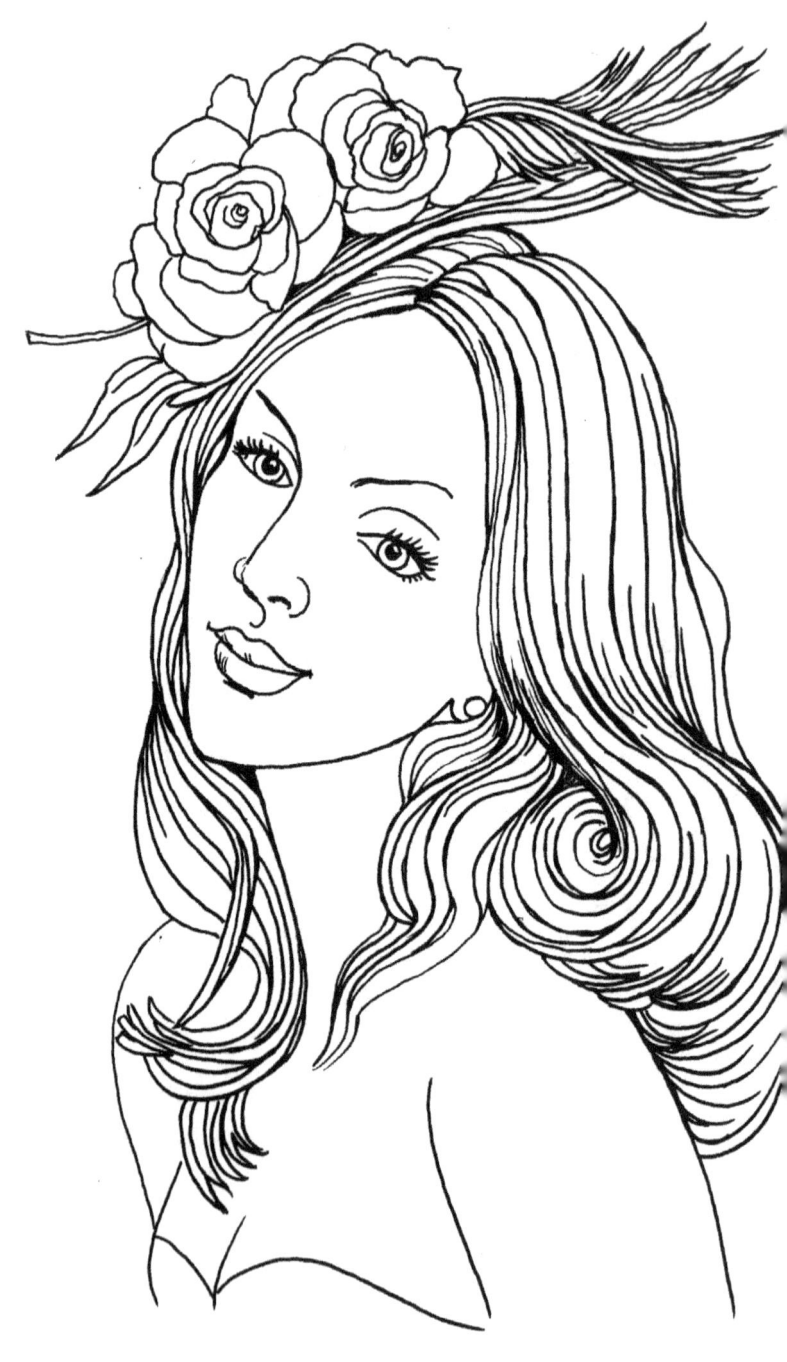

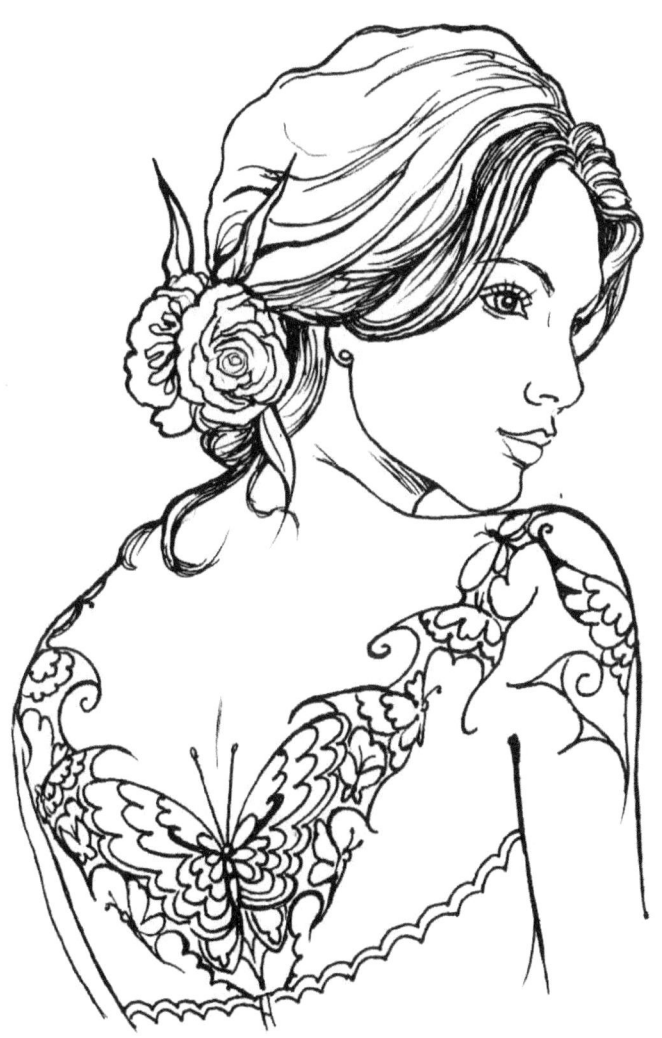

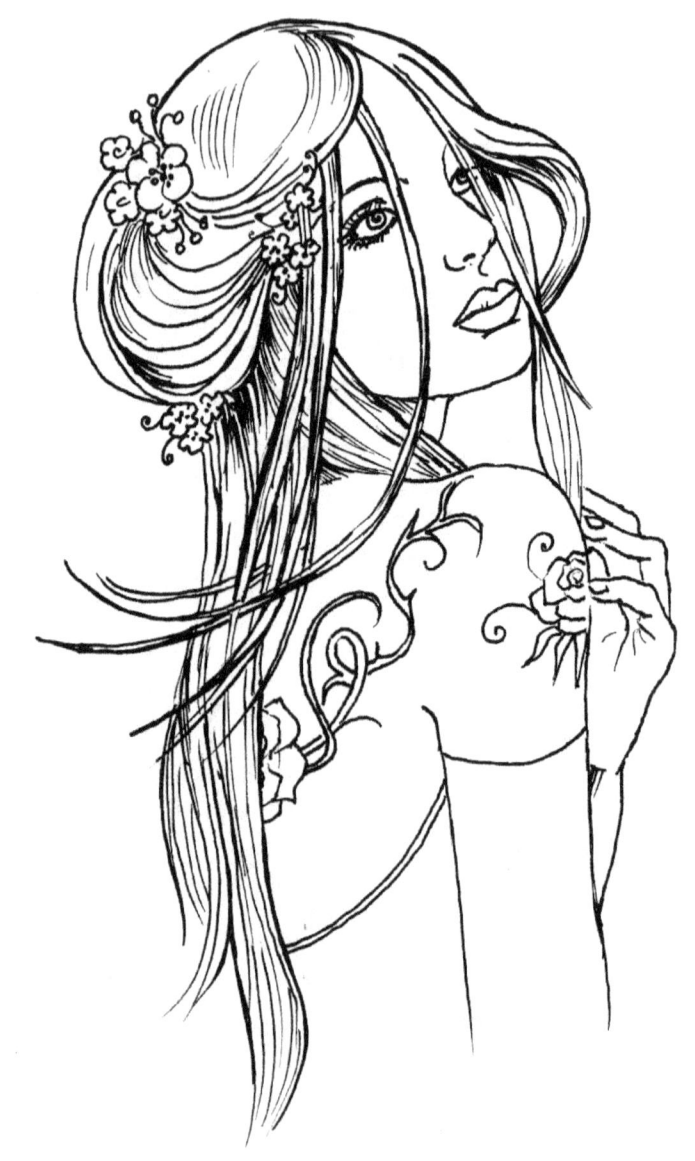

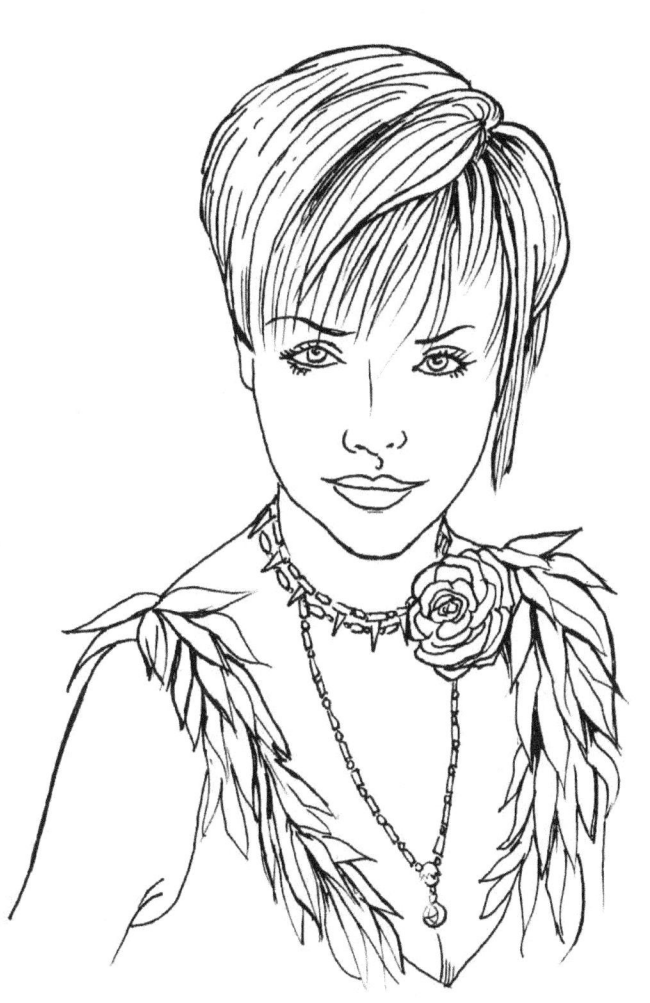

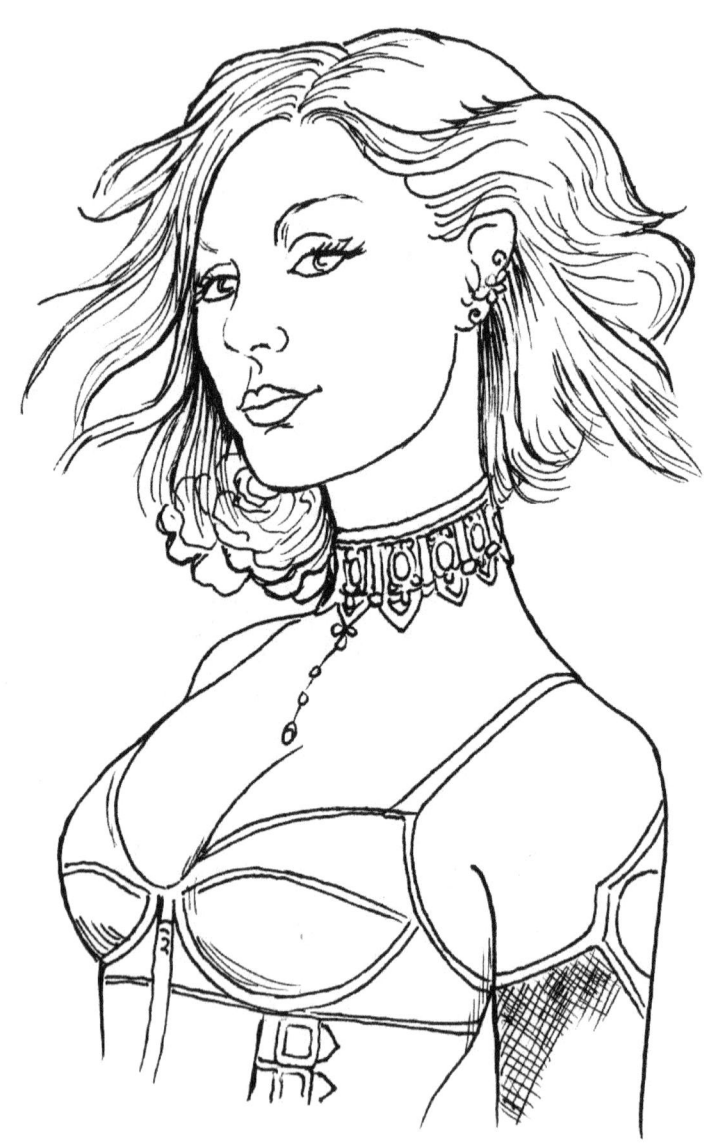

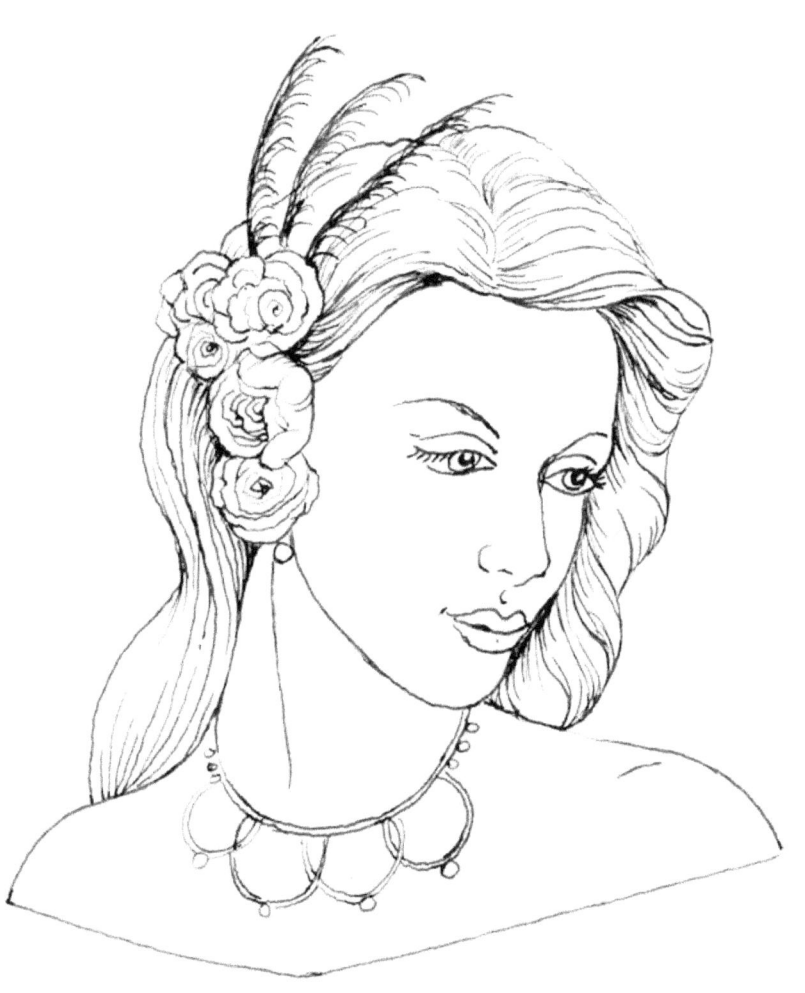

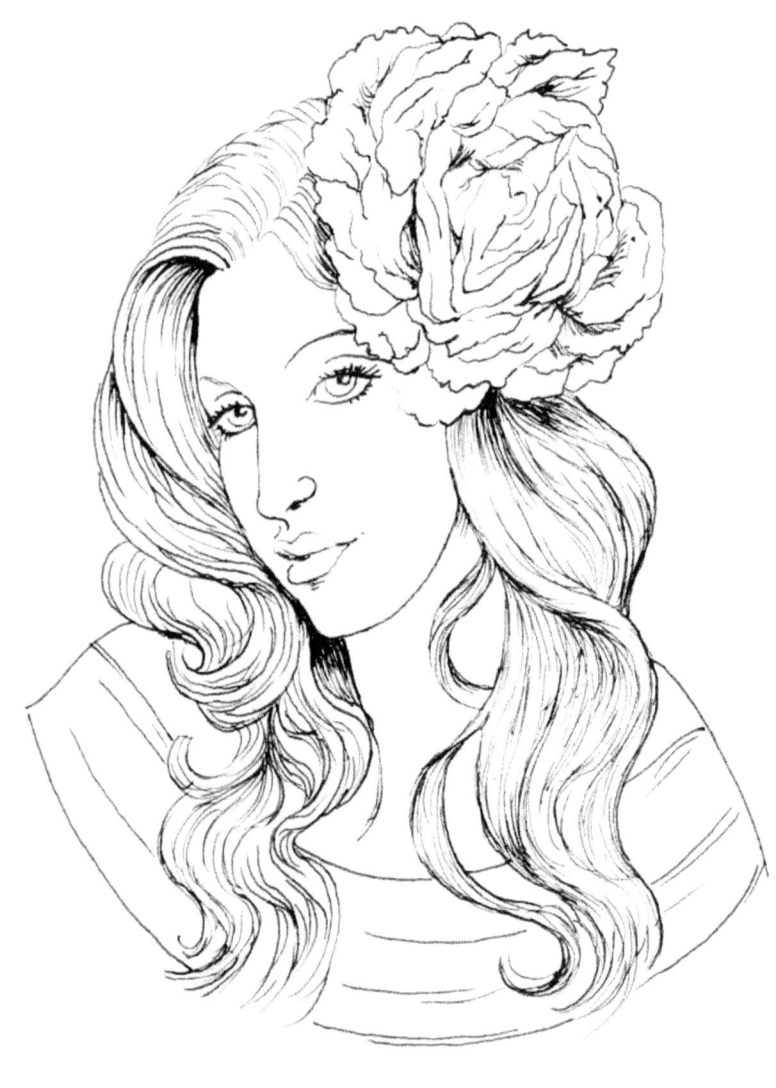

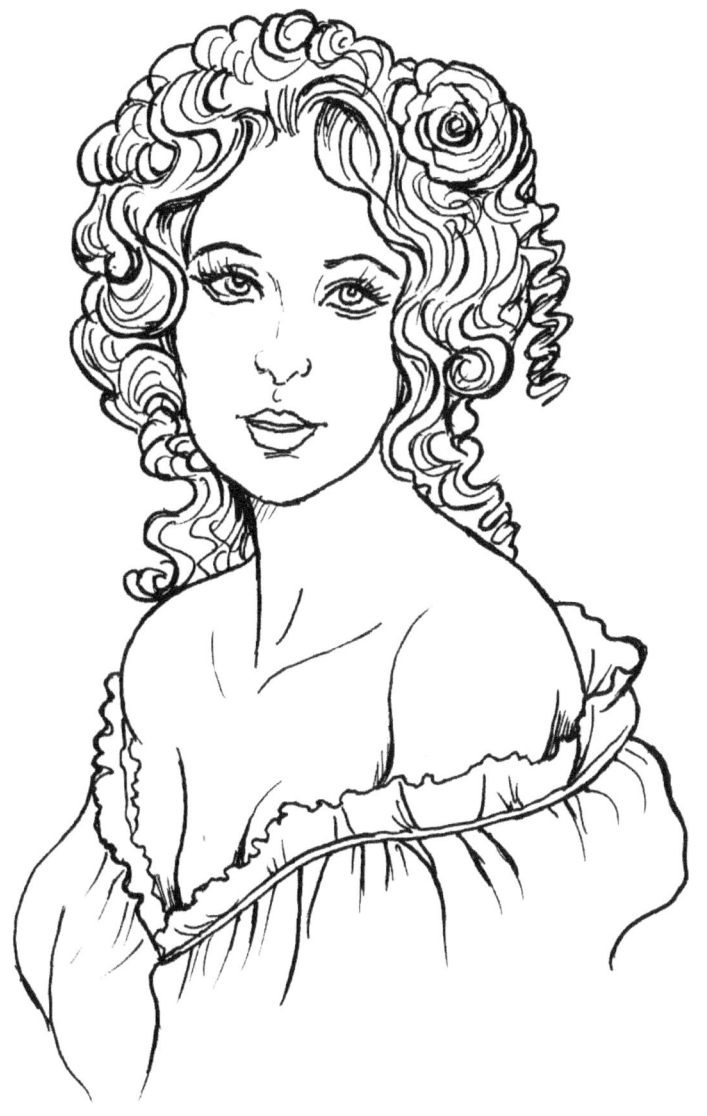

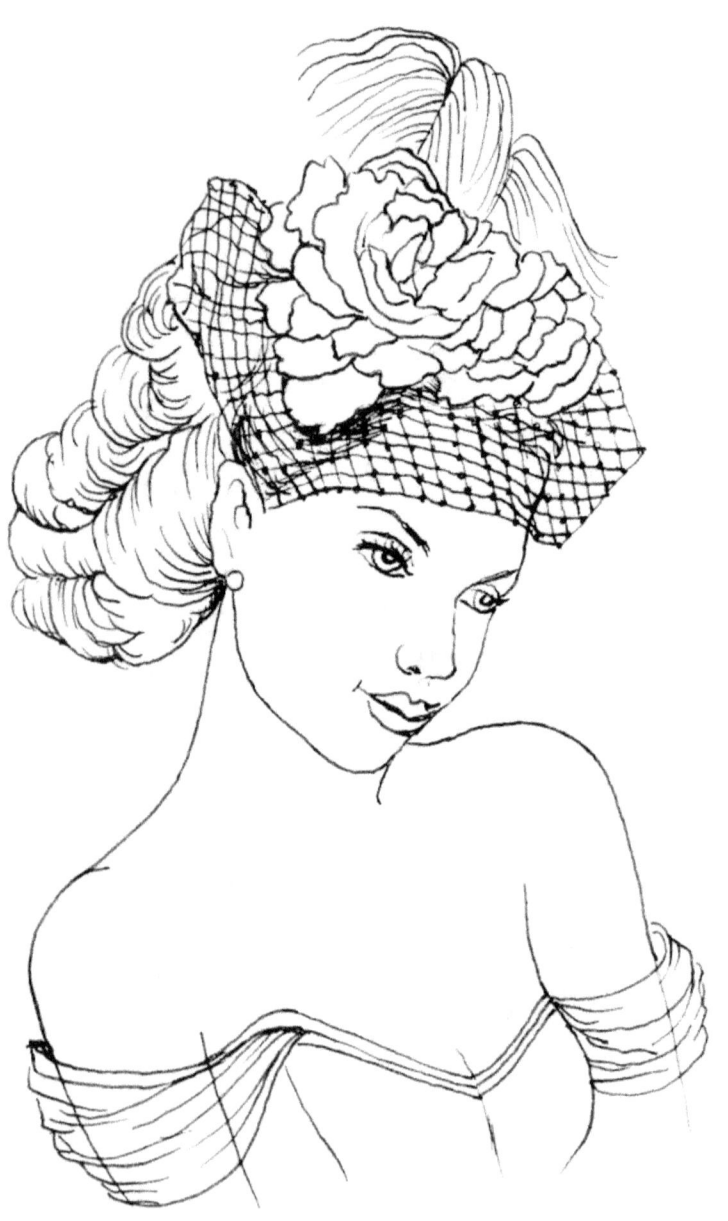

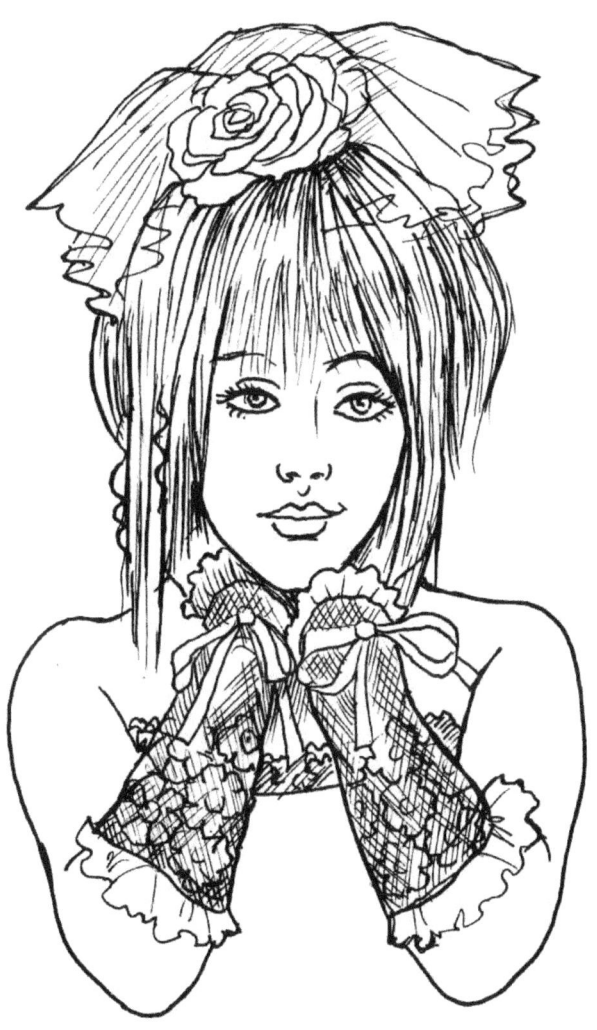

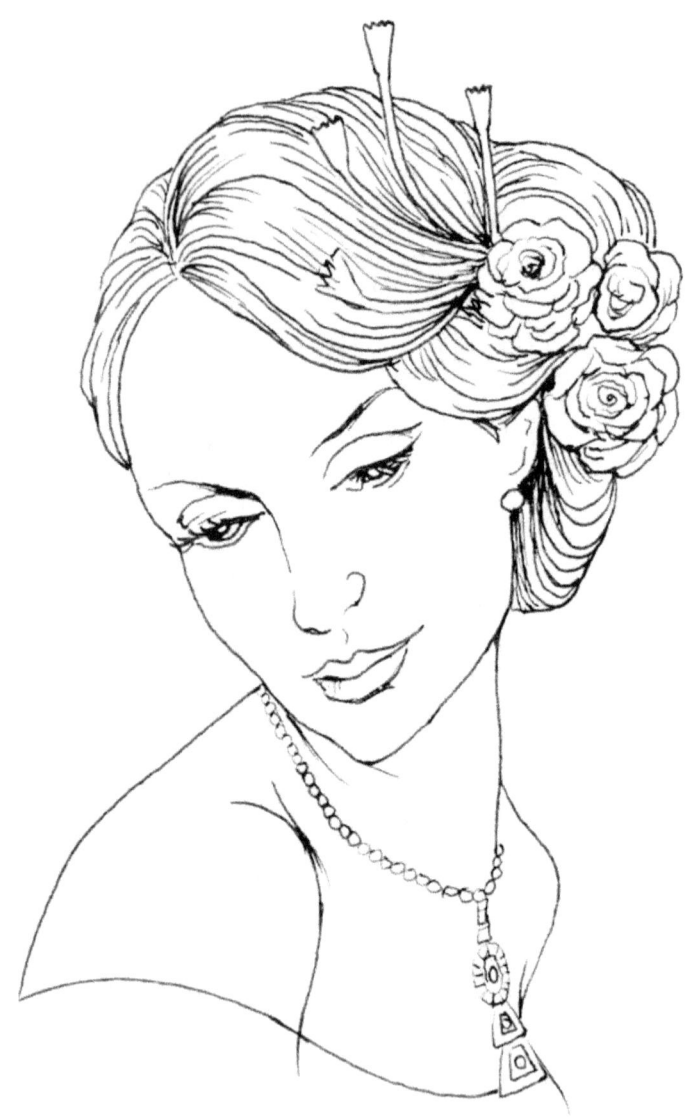

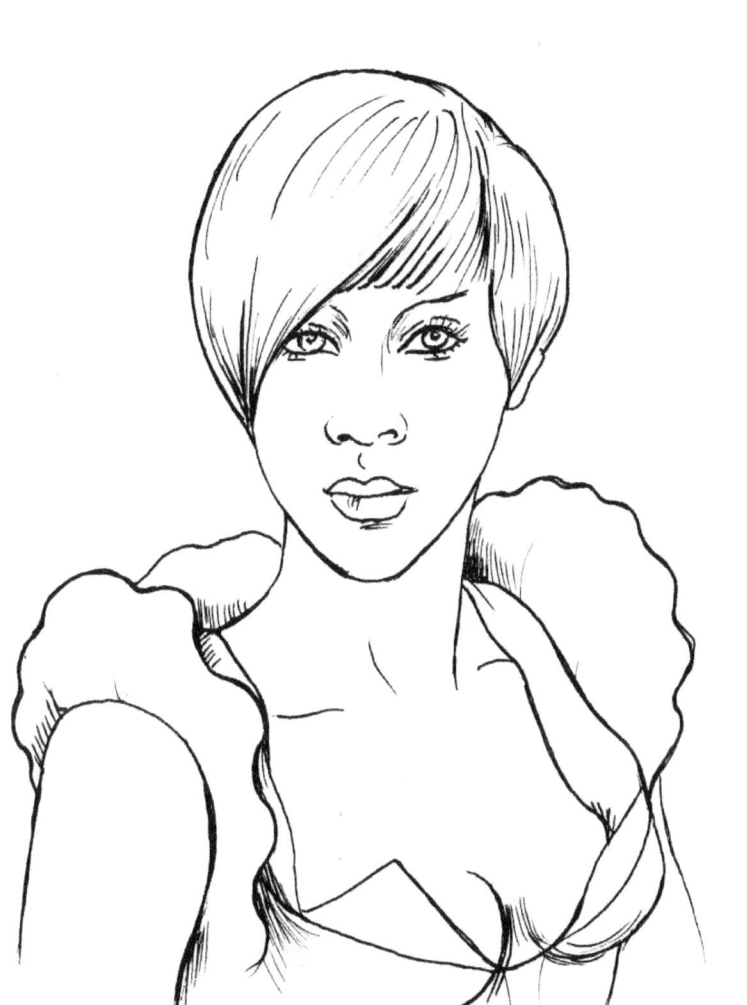

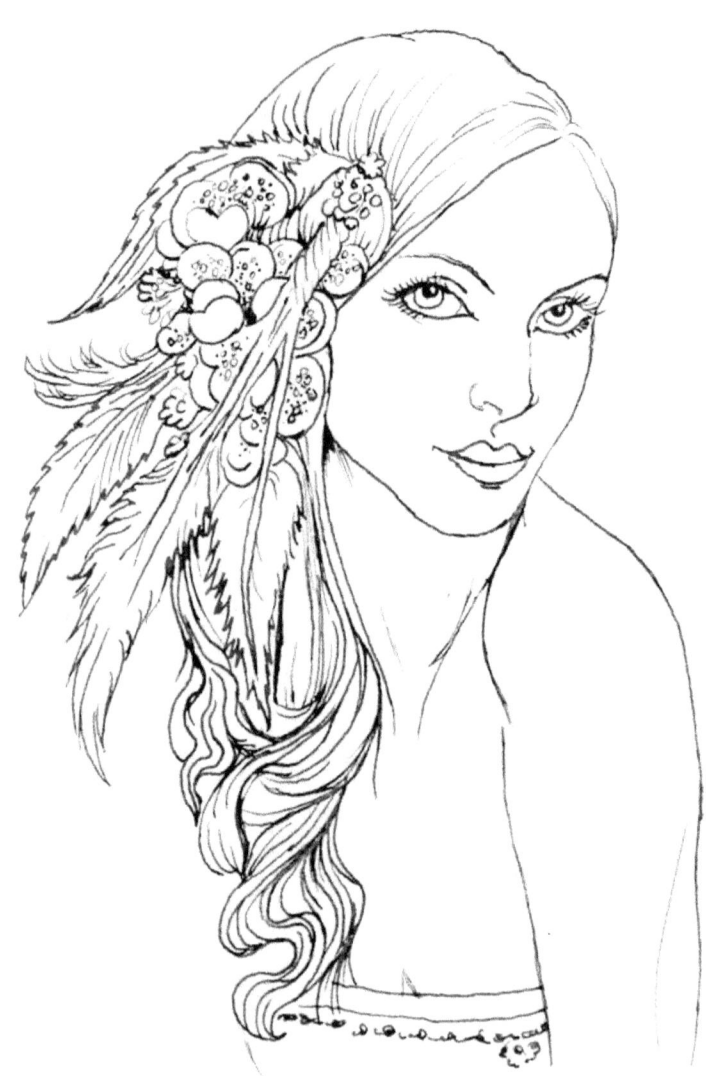

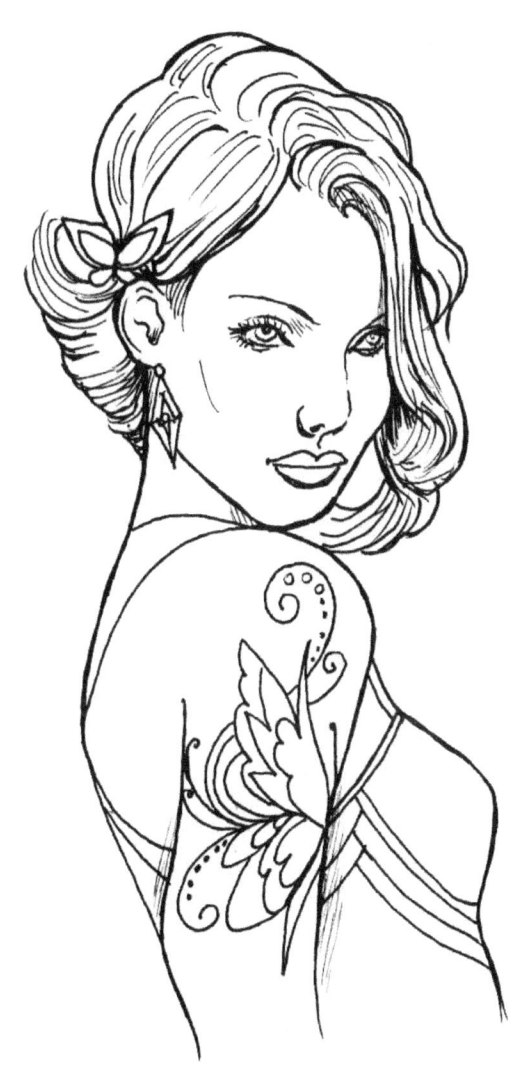

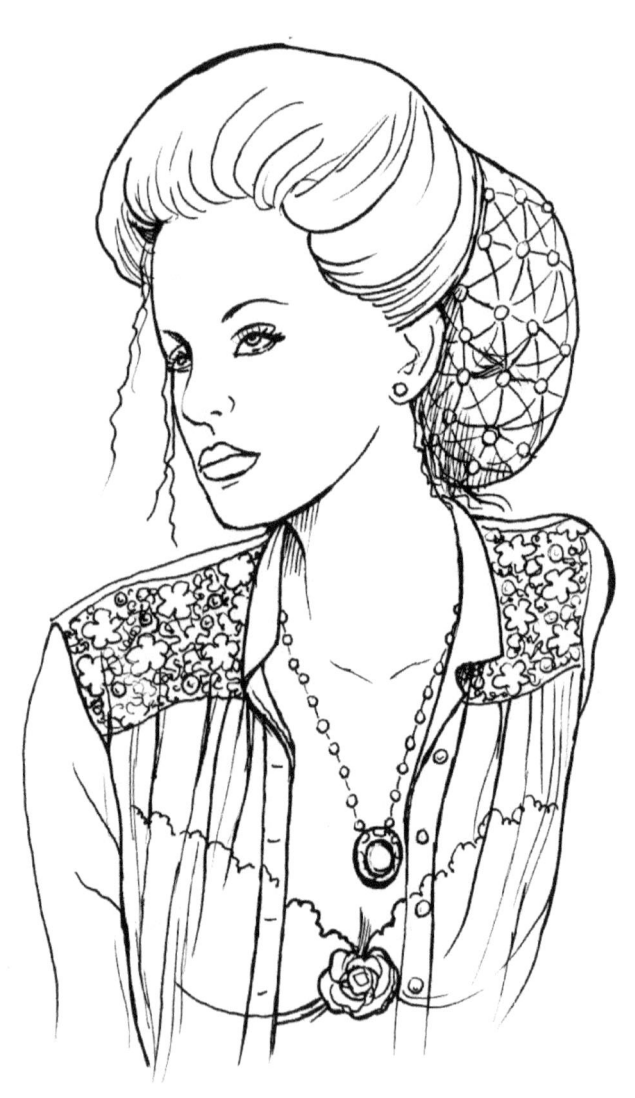

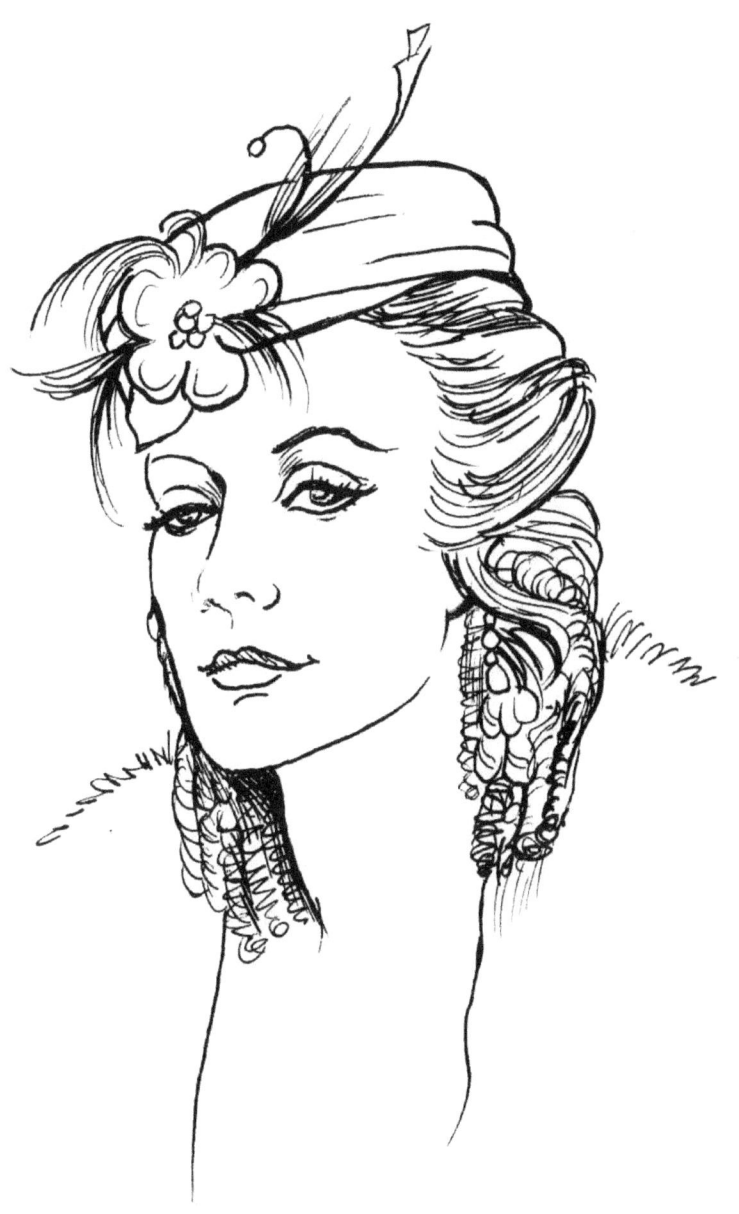

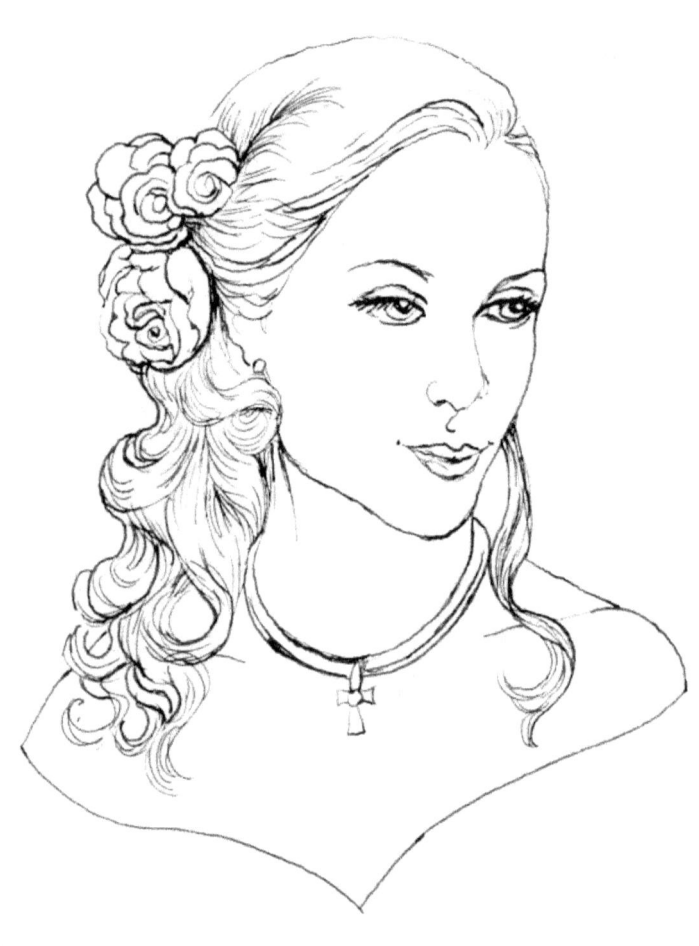

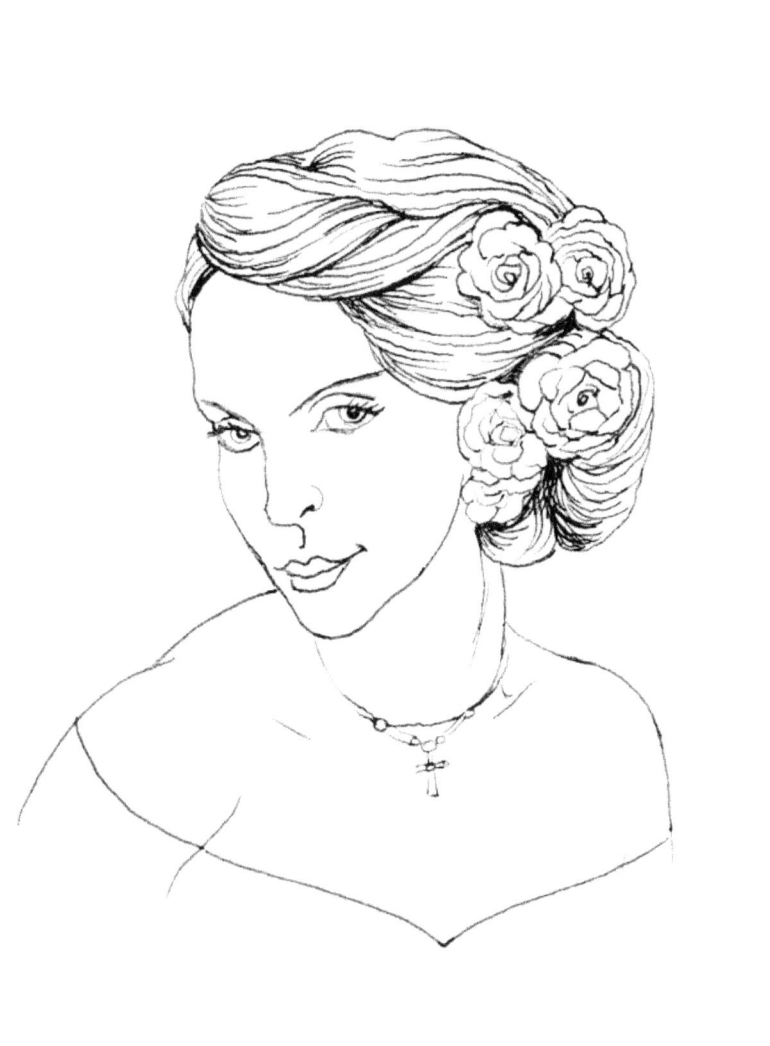

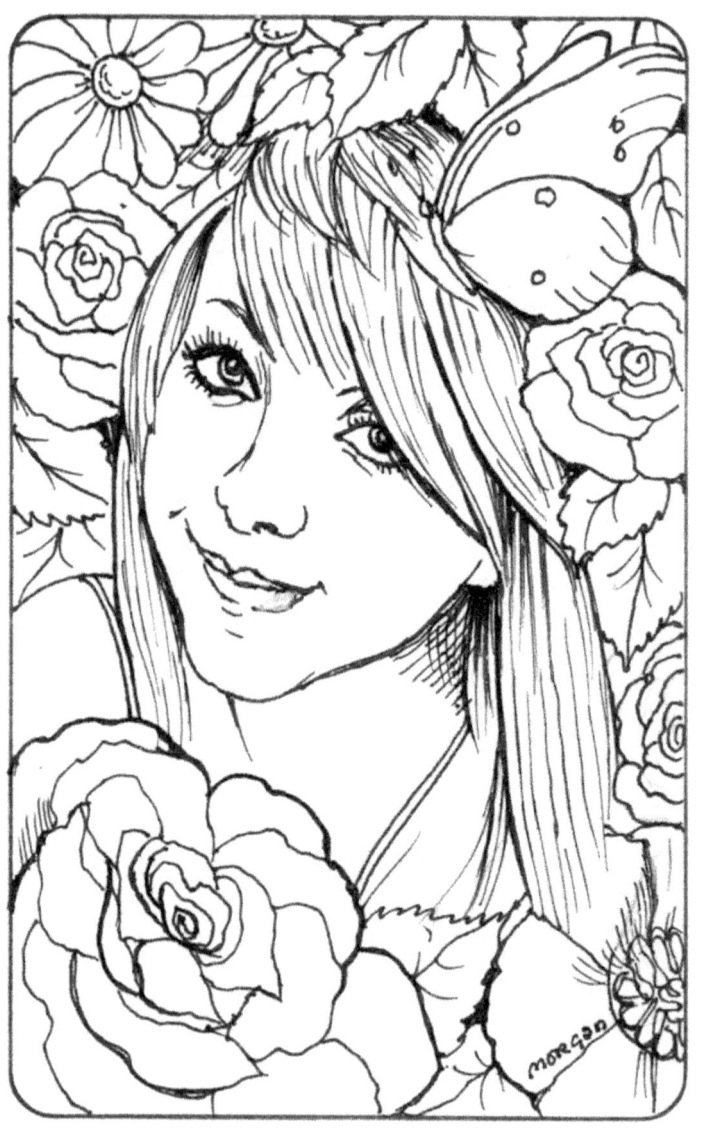

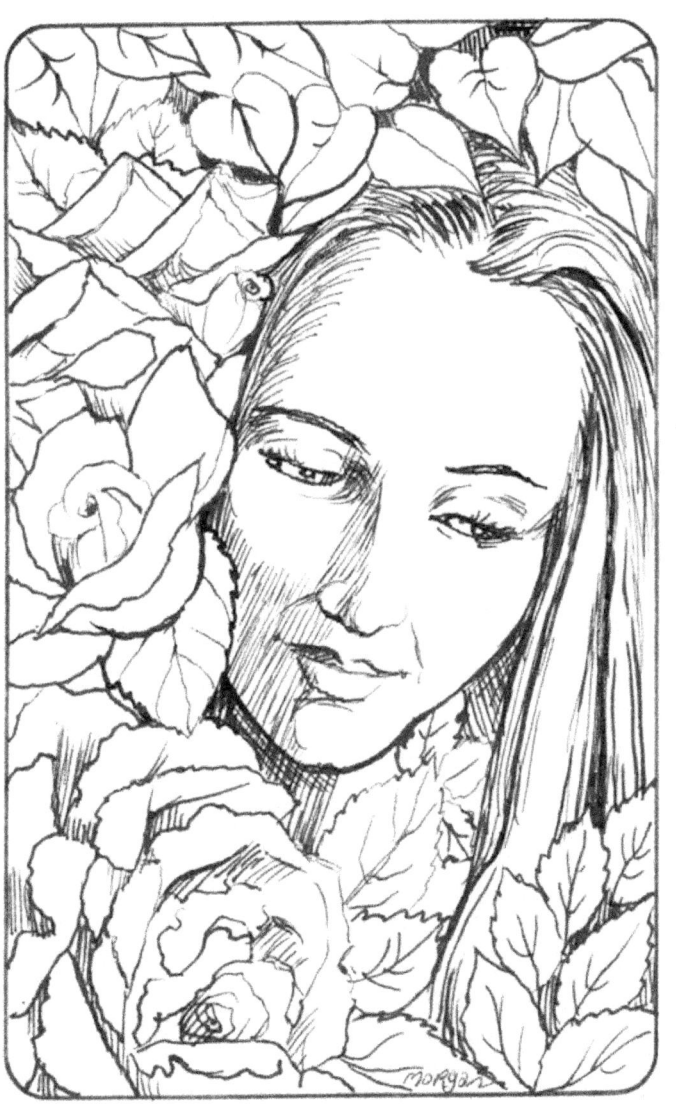

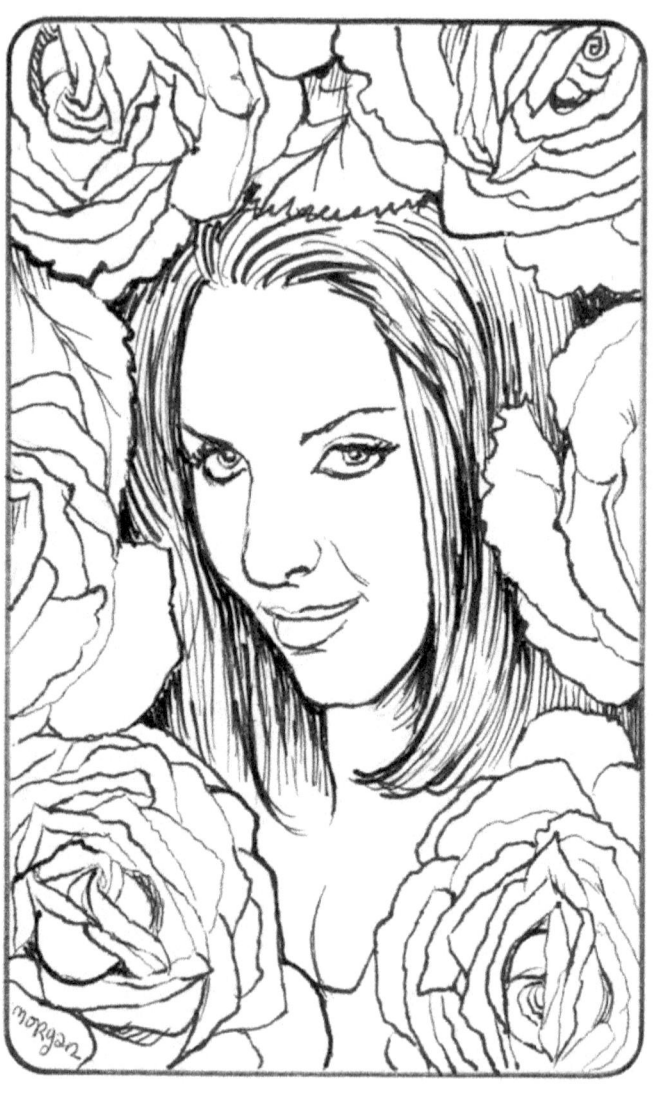

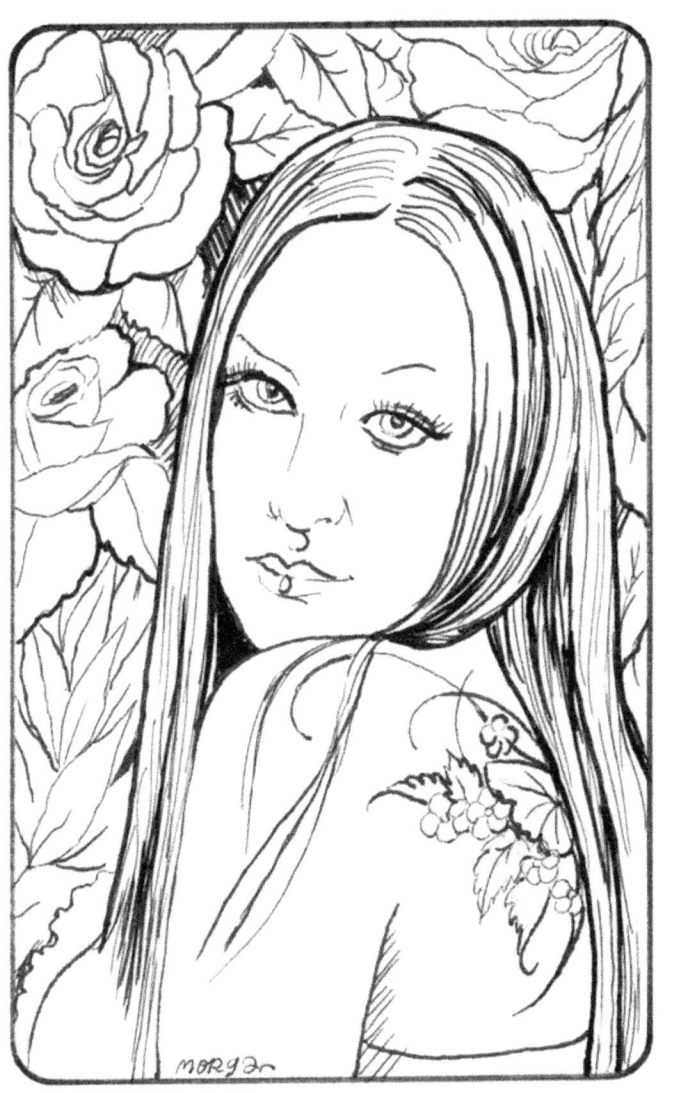

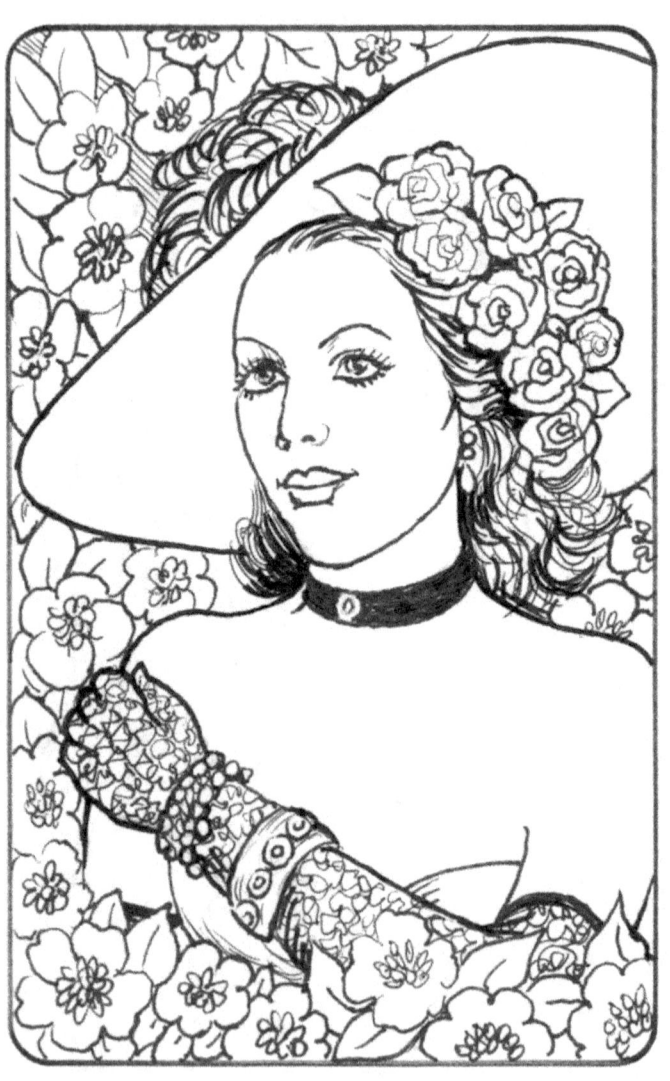

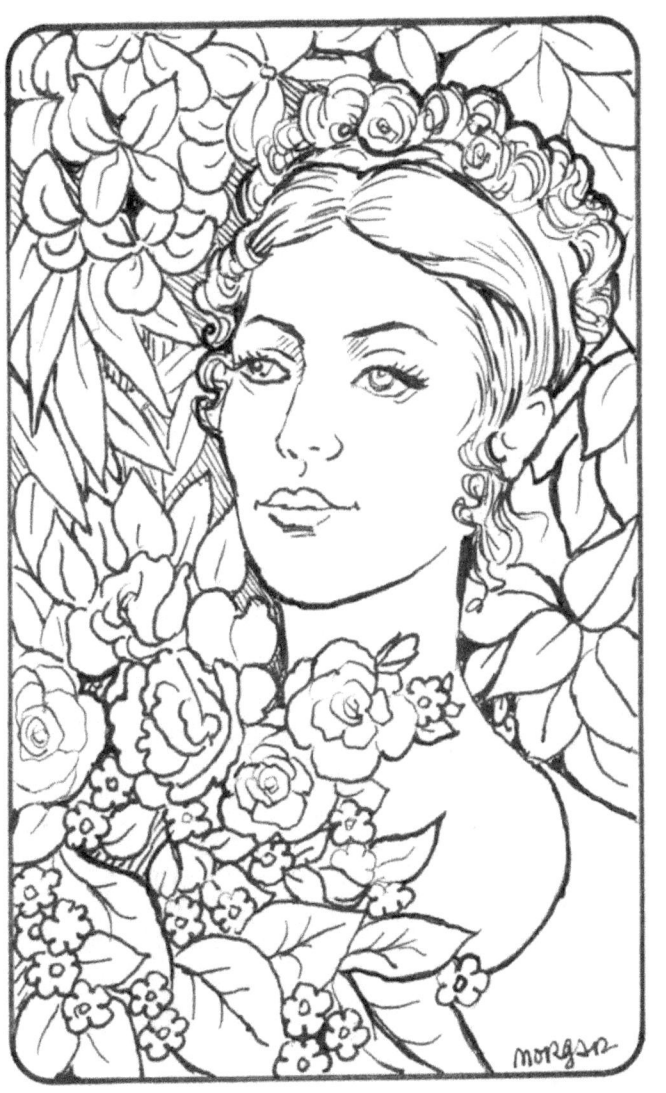

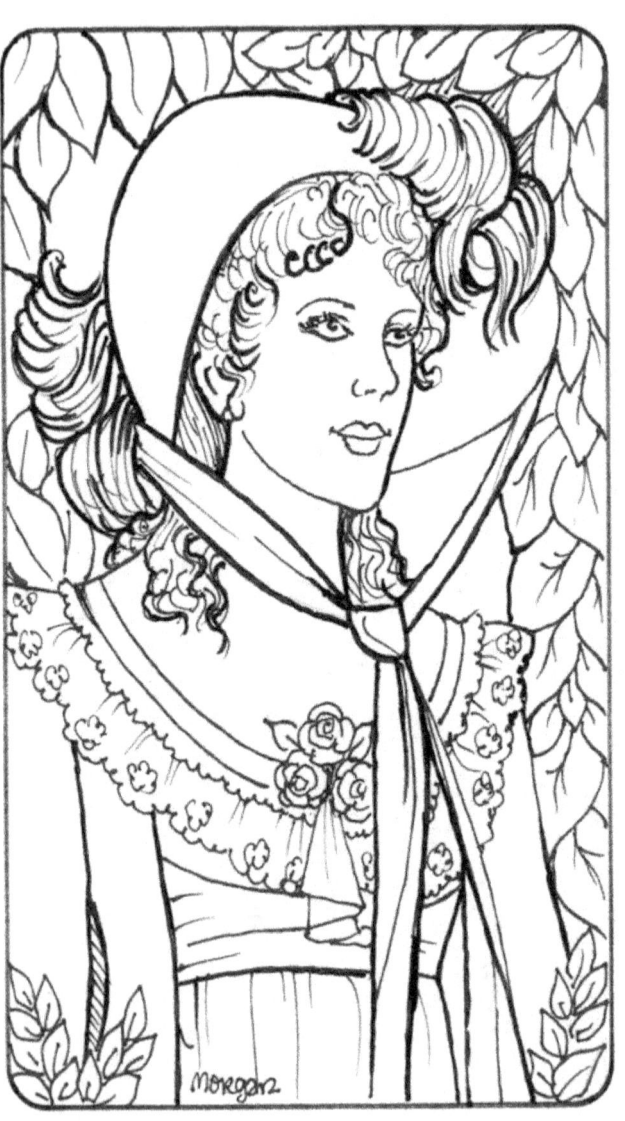

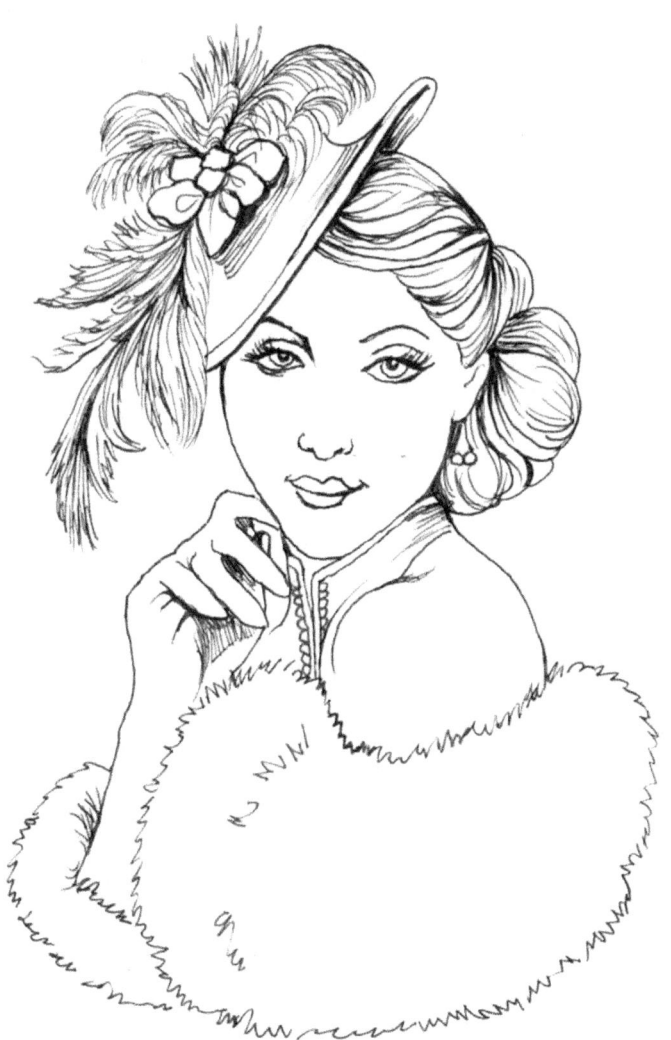

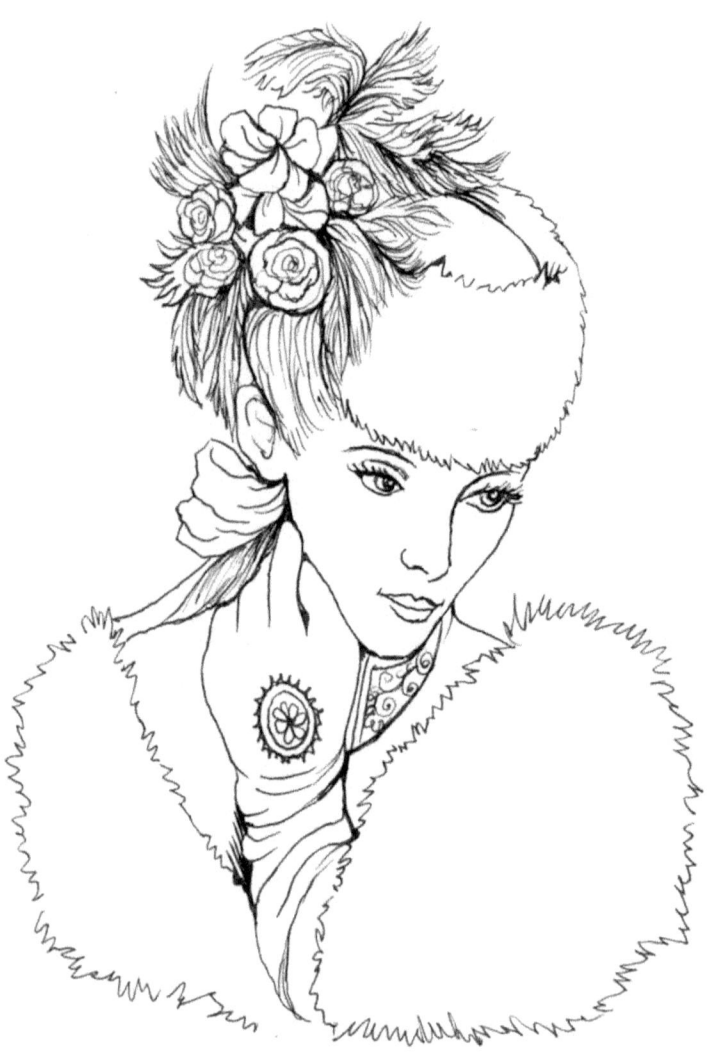

www.ingramcontent.com/pod-product-compliance
Lightning Source LLC
Chambersburg PA
CBHW070959220526
45471CB00007B/3106